The Old Man and the Sea

by Ernest Hemingway

Level 3
(1600-word)

Adapted by Roland Kelts

JN094941

IBC パブリッシング

はじめに

　ラダーシリーズは、「はしご（ladder）」を使って一歩一歩上を目指すように、学習者の実力に合わせ、無理なくステップアップできるよう開発された英文リーダーのシリーズです。

　リーディング力をつけるためには、繰り返したくさん読むこと、いわゆる「多読」がもっとも効果的な学習法であると言われています。多読では、「1. 速く 2. 訳さず英語のまま 3. なるべく辞書を使わず」に読むことが大切です。スピードを計るなど、速く読むよう心がけましょう（たとえば TOEIC® テストの音声スピードはおよそ 1 分間に 150 語です）。そして 1 語ずつ訳すのではなく、英語を英語のまま理解するくせをつけるようにします。こうして読み続けるうちに語感がついてきて、だんだんと英語が理解できるようになるのです。まずは、ラダーシリーズの中からあなたのレベルに合った本を選び、少しずつ英文に慣れ親しんでください。たくさんの本を手にとるうちに、英文書がすらすら読めるようになってくるはずです。

《**本シリーズの特徴**》

- 中学校レベルから中級者レベルまで５段階に分かれています。自分に合ったレベルからスタートしてください。

- クラシックから現代文学、ノンフィクション、ビジネスと幅広いジャンルを扱っています。あなたの興味に合わせてタイトルを選べます。

- 巻末のワードリストで、いつでもどこでも単語の意味を確認できます。レベル１、２では、文中の全ての単語が、レベル３以上は中学校レベル外の単語が掲載されています。

- カバーにヘッドホーンマークのついているタイトルは、オーディオ・サポートがあります。ウェブから購入／ダウンロードし、リスニング教材としても併用できます。

《**使用語彙について**》

レベル１：中学校で学習する単語約 1000 語

レベル２：レベル１の単語＋使用頻度の高い単語約 300 語

レベル３：レベル１の単語＋使用頻度の高い単語約 600 語

レベル４：レベル１の単語＋使用頻度の高い単語約 1000 語

レベル５：語彙制限なし

The Old Man
and the Sea

読みはじめる前に

【登場人物】　Santiago　サンチャゴ《老漁師の名》
　　　　　　　Manolin　マノーリン《少年の名》

【魚の名】
albacore　ビンナガ（マグロ）
barracuda　バラクーダ
dolphin　シイラ
flying fish　トビウオ
Mako shark　アオザメ
marlin　マカジキ
porpoise　ネズミイルカ

sardine　イワシ
shovel-nosed shark　シャベルのような鼻をしたサメ（ニシレモンザメのこと）
sucking fish　コバンザメ
swordfish　メカジキ
tuna　マグロ

【魚の部位など】
bill　くちばし
carcass　残骸, 死骸
dorsal fin　背びれ
fin　ひれ

gill　えら
gut　はらわた
hide　皮
spear　槍, 吻（ふん）

【漁具関連】
cast net　投網
fishing line　釣り糸
gaff　魚鉤（かぎ）, やす
gear　用具, 装具

harpoon　銛（もり）
leader　はりす《釣り針を結んでいる短い釣り糸》
noose　輪なわ

【船関連】
bow　船首
mast　マスト
oar　オール, 櫂（かい）
planking　板張り

rudder　舵（かじ）
stern　船尾
tiller　舵の柄
tow　曳航する

An old man who fished alone had gone 84 days without catching a fish. In the first forty days, a boy had been with him. But after forty days without a fish, the boy's parents had told him that the old man was not lucky, so the boy had gone to another boat.

It made the boy sad to see the old man come in each day with his boat empty, and he always went down to help him carry things. The boat's sail was held together with old sacks. It looked like a flag of defeat.

The old man was thin with deep wrinkles in the back of his neck. Brown spots of skin cancer were on his cheeks. The spots ran down the sides of his face, and his hands had deep scars from handling heavy fish. None of the scars were fresh.

Everything about him was old except his eyes. They were the same color as the sea and were cheerful and undefeated.

"Santiago," the boy said to him. "I could go with you again. We've made some money."

The old man had taught the boy to fish, and the boy loved him.

"No," the old man said. "You're with a lucky boat. Stay with them."

"But remember how you went 87 days without fish, and then we caught big ones every day for three weeks?"

"I remember," the old man said. "I know you did not leave me because you doubted."

"It was papa who made me leave."

"I know," the old man said.

"Can I offer you a beer on the Terrace before we take the stuff home?" the boy asked.

"Why not?" the old man said. "Between fishermen."

Many of the successful fishermen made fun

of the old man, but he was not angry. The older fishermen looked at him and were sad, but they did not show it.

"Santiago," the boy said. "Can I go out to get sardines for you for tomorrow?"

"No. Go and play baseball. I can still row, and Rogelio will throw the net."

"I would like to go. If I cannot fish with you, I would still like to help you somehow."

"You bought me a beer," the old man said. "You are already a man."

"How old was I when you first took me in a boat?"

"Five, and you were nearly killed when I brought the fish in too quickly and he nearly tore the boat to pieces. Can you remember?"

"I can remember the tail slapping and banging and the noise. I can remember you throwing me into the bow where the wet lines were and feeling the whole boat shake, and the noise of you clubbing him like chopping a tree, and the sweet smell of blood all over me."

"Can you really remember that or did I just tell you?"

"I remember everything from when we first went together."

The old man looked at him with loving eyes.

"If you were my boy I'd take you out and gamble," he said. "But you are your father's and your mother's and you are in a lucky boat."

"May I get the sardines? I know where I can get four baits too."

"I have mine left from today."

"Let me get four fresh ones."

"One," the old man said. His hope and his confidence had never gone.

"Two," the boy said.

"Two," the old man agreed. "You didn't take them?"

"I would," the boy said. "But I bought these."

"Thank you," the old man said.

"Tomorrow is going to be a good day with

this current," he said.

"Where are you going?" the boy asked.

"Far out to sea. I want to be out before it is light."

"I'll try to get him to work far out," the boy said. "Then if you catch something truly big we can help you."

"He does not like to work too far out."

"No," the boy said. "But I will say I see something that he cannot see such as a bird working and get him to come out after dolphin."

"Are his eyes that bad?"

"He cannot see."

"It is strange," the old man said. "He never went turtle fishing. That is what kills the eyes."

"But you went turtle fishing for years off the Mosquito Coast and your eyes are good."

"I am a strange old man."

"But are you strong enough now for a truly big fish?"

"I think so."

"Let us take the stuff home," the boy said, "so I can get the cast net and go after the sardines."

They picked up the gear from the boat. The old man carried the mast on his shoulder, and the boy carried the wooden box with the coiled brown lines, the gaff, and the harpoon.

They walked up the road to the old man's shack and went inside through its open door. There used to be a photo of the old man's wife on the wall but he took it down because it made him feel lonely.

These days, the old man dreamed of lions in Africa. The lions were young and played together at sunset.

The old man loved the lions as much as he loved the boy. But he never dreamed about the boy. He just woke up, looked at the moon in the sky outside his open door, and put his pants on. Then he went up the road to wake up the boy.

When they walked back to the old man's shack, the boy took the fishing line from the basket and grabbed the harpoon and gaff, while the old man carried the mast with the folded sail on his shoulder.

Then they went out and had coffee at an early morning place that served fishermen.

"How did you sleep old man?" the boy asked. He was waking up now although it was still hard for him to leave his sleep.

"Very well, Manolin," he said. "I feel confident today."

"So do I," the boy said. "Now I must get your sardines and mine and your fresh baits. He brings our gear himself. He never wants anyone to carry anything."

"We're different," the old man said. "I let you carry things when you were five years old."

"I know it," the boy said. "I'll be right back. Have another coffee. We have credit here."

He walked off, bare-footed on the coral

rocks, to the icehouse where the baits were stored.

The old man drank his coffee slowly. It was all he would have all day and he knew that he should drink it. He had a bottle of water in the bow of the boat and that was all he needed for the day.

The boy was back now with the sardines and the two baits wrapped in a newspaper and they went down to the boat, and they lifted the boat and slid it into the water.

"Good luck old man."

The old man knew he was going far out to sea. He left the smell of the land behind and rowed out into the clean early morning smell of the ocean.

In the dark the old man could feel the morning coming, and as he rowed he heard the sound as flying fish left the water and the beating of their wings as they flew away in the darkness.

As it started to be light he saw he was already further out than he had hoped to be at this hour.

He watched the dip of the three sticks over the side of the boat and rowed gently to keep the lines straight up and down and at their depths. He kept them straighter than anyone did, so that at each level in the darkness of the stream, there would be bait waiting exactly where he wished it to be for any fish that swam there.

I keep them with care, he thought. Only I have no luck any more. But who knows? Maybe today. Every day is a new day. It is better to be lucky. But I would rather be exact. Then when luck comes you are ready.

Just then he saw a man-of-war bird with his long black wings circling in the sky ahead of him. He made a quick drop, slanting down on his wings, and then circled again.

"He's got something," the old man said

aloud. "He's not just looking."

He rowed slowly toward where the bird was circling. He did not hurry and he kept his lines straight up and down.

The bird went higher in the air and circled again, his wings motionless. Then he dove suddenly and the old man saw flying fish jump out of the water and sail desperately over the surface.

"Dolphin," the old man said aloud. "Big dolphin."

Now the old man looked up and saw that the bird was circling again.

"He's found fish," he said aloud. As the old man watched, a small tuna rose in the air, turned and dropped head first into the water. The tuna shone silver in the sun, and after he had dropped back into the water, another and another rose and they were jumping in all directions, leaping in long jumps after the bait.

"The bird is a great help," the old man said.

Just then the stern line got tighter under his foot, where he had kept a loop of the line, and he dropped his oars and felt the weight of the small tuna's pull as he held the line firm and pulled it in.

"Albacore," he said aloud. "He'll make a beautiful bait."

He did not remember when he had first started to talk aloud when he was by himself. He had probably started to talk aloud after the boy had left.

The sun was hot now, and the old man felt it on the back of his neck, and felt the sweat on his back as he rowed.

Just then, watching his lines, he saw one of the green sticks dip sharply.

"Yes," he said.

The old man held the line with his left hand and took it off the stick. Now he could let it run through his fingers without the fish feeling any tension.

He felt the light pulling and then a harder pull. Then there was nothing.

"Come on," the old man said aloud.

He waited with the line between his thumb and his finger, watching it and the other lines.

"He'll take the line," the old man said aloud. "God help him to take it."

He did not take it though. He was gone and the old man felt nothing.

Then he felt the gentle touch on the line and he was happy.

He was happy feeling the gentle pulling and then he felt something hard and heavy. It was the weight of the fish and he let the line slip down. As it went down, slipping through the old man's fingers, he could still feel the great weight.

"What a fish," he said. "He has it sideways in his mouth now and he is moving off with it."

Then he will turn and swallow it, he thought. He did not say that because he knew that if you said a good thing, it might not happen. Then the weight increased and he gave more line.

"He's taken it," he said. "Now I'll let him eat it well."

Eat it so that the point of the hook goes into your heart and kills you, he thought. Come up easy and let me put the harpoon into you.

"Now!" he said aloud and struck hard with both hands, gained a yard of line and then struck again and again with each arm on the line and all the strength of his arms and the weight of his body.

Nothing happened. The fish just moved away slowly and the old man could not raise him an inch. The boat began to move slowly off toward the northwest.

The fish moved and they traveled slowly on the water. The other baits were still in the water but there was nothing to be done.

"I wish I had the boy," the old man said

aloud. "I'm being pulled in my boat by a fish."

What I will do if he decides to go down, I don't know. But I'll do something. There are many things I can do.

He held the line against his back and watched its slant in the water and the boat moving to the northwest.

This will kill him, the old man thought. He can't do this forever. But four hours later the fish was still swimming out to sea, towing the boat, and the old man still had the line across his back.

"It was noon when I hooked him," he said. "And I still haven't seen him."

He had pushed his straw hat hard down on his head before he hooked the fish and it was cutting his forehead. Then he looked behind him and saw that no land was visible. That makes no difference, he thought. There are two more hours before sunset and maybe he will come up before that.

The fish never changed course or direction that night as far as the man could tell from watching the stars. It was cold after the sun went down and the old man's sweat dried cold on his back and his arms and his old legs.

I can do nothing with him and he can do nothing with me, he thought. Not as long as he keeps this up.

Once he stood up and peed over the side of the boat and looked at the stars and checked his course. He knew the current must be carrying them to the eastward.

Then he said aloud, "I wish I had the boy. To help me and to see this."

No one should be alone when they are old, he thought. But it is unavoidable. I must remember to eat the tuna in order to keep strong.

During the night, two porpoises came around the boat and he could hear them rolling and blowing.

"They are good," he said. "They play and love one another. They are our brothers, like the flying fish."

Then he began to feel sorry for the great fish that he had caught. He is wonderful and strange and who knows how old he is, he thought.

"I wish the boy was here," he said aloud and settled himself against the rounded wood of the bow and felt the strength of the great fish through the line he held across his shoulders.

The fish suddenly pulled hard on the line and made him fall down on his face, where he got cut below his eye. The blood ran down his cheek. But it dried before it reached his chin, and he worked his way back to the bow and rested against the wood.

"Fish," he said softly, aloud, "I'll stay with you until I am dead."

He'll stay with me too, I suppose, the old man thought, and he waited for it to be light. It was cold now in the time before daylight and he pushed against the wood to be warm.

"He's headed north," the old man said. The current will have set us far to the eastward, he thought. I wish he would turn with the current. That would show that he was tiring.

When the sun had risen further, the old man realized that the fish was not tiring. There was only one favorable sign. The slant of the line showed he was swimming at a lesser depth. That did not necessarily mean that he would jump. But he might.

"Fish," he said, "I love you and respect you very much. But I will kill you before this day ends."

Just then the fish moved suddenly and pulled the old man down to the bow. The fish would have pulled him overboard if he had not grabbed the edge of the boat and given the fish some line.

He felt the line carefully with his right hand

and noticed his hand was bloody.

"Something hurt him then," he said aloud. He pulled back on the line to see if he could turn the fish. But when he was touching the breaking point he held on and settled back against the line.

"You're feeling it now, fish," he said. "And so, God knows, am I."

How did I let the fish cut me with that one quick pull he made? I must be getting very stupid. Now I will pay attention to my work and then I must eat the tuna so that I will not lose my strength.

"I wish the boy were here and that I had some salt," he said aloud.

Shifting the weight of the line to his left shoulder and kneeling carefully he washed his hand in the ocean and held it there, submerged, for more than a minute, watching the blood and the movement of the water against his hand as the boat moved.

"He has slowed much," he said.

The old man would have liked to keep his hand in the salt water longer, but he was afraid of another sudden lurch by the fish, and he stood up and braced himself and held his hand up against the sun.

"Now," he said, when his hand had dried, "I must eat the small tuna. I can reach him with the gaff and eat him here."

He knelt down and found the tuna under the stern and drew it toward him. Holding the line with his left shoulder again, and bracing on his left hand and arm, he took the tuna off the line. He put one knee on the fish and cut dark red meat from the back of the head to the tail. He cut meat from next to the back bone down to the edge of the belly. When he had cut six pieces he spread them out on the wood of the bow, wiped his knife on his pants, and lifted the carcass of the tuna by the tail and dropped it overboard.

"I don't think I can eat an entire one," he said. He could feel the hard pull of the line and his left hand was cramped.

"What kind of a hand is that," he said. "Cramp then if you want. Make yourself into a claw. It will do you no good."

He picked up a piece of tuna and put it in his mouth and chewed it slowly. It was not bad.

Chew it well, he thought, and get all the juices.

"How do you feel, hand?" he asked his cramped hand. "I'll eat some more for you."

He ate the other part of the piece that he had cut in two. He chewed it carefully and then spat out the skin.

"How does it go, hand? Or is it too early to know?"

He took another full piece and chewed it.

"It is a strong full-blooded fish," he thought. "I was lucky to get him instead of a dolphin. Dolphin meat is too sweet. This is hardly sweet at all and all the strength is still in it."

I wish I could feed the fish, he thought. He is my brother. But I must kill him and keep strong to do it. He ate all of the tuna.

He straightened up.

"God, please help me to stop this cramp," he said. "Because I do not know what the fish is going to do."

He pressed the cramped hand against his pants and tried to open his fingers. But they would not open.

He looked across the sea and knew how alone he was now.

If there is a hurricane, you always see the signs of it in the sky for days ahead if you are at sea. They do not see it on land because they do not know what to look for, he thought. But we have no hurricane coming now.

He looked at the sky and saw the big white clouds stacked like ice cream in the September sky.

His left hand was still cramped, but he was opening it slowly.

I hate this cramp, he thought. If the boy were here he could help me. But it will get better.

Then, with his right hand, he felt the difference in the pull of the line before he saw the slant change in the water.

"He's coming up," he said.

The line rose slowly and then the surface of the ocean rose ahead of the boat and the fish came out of the water. He was bright in the sun, and his head and back were dark purple, and in the sun the stripes on his sides were wide and a light lavender color.

The old man had seen many great fish. He had seen many that were more than a thousand pounds and he had caught two of that size in his life, but never alone.

There was a small sea rising with the wind coming up from the east and at noon the old man's left hand was not cramped.

"Bad news for you, fish," he said, and shifted the line over the sacks that covered his shoulders.

"I am not religious," he said. "But I will say twenty prayers if I catch this fish. That is a promise."

The sun was hot now although the breeze was rising gently.

It was getting into the afternoon and the boat still moved slowly. But there was a breeze and the old man rode gently on the small sea. Now that he had seen him once, he could picture the fish swimming in the water.

The movement of his fingers had relaxed his left hand now, and he began to shift more of the line to his left hand, and he shrugged the muscles of his back to make the line hurt less.

He felt very tired now, and he knew the night would come soon and he tried to think of other things.

"Unless sharks come," he said aloud.

Just before it was dark, his smaller fishing line caught a dolphin. He saw it first when it jumped in the air. It jumped again and again in fear, and he worked his way to the back of the boat. Crouching and holding the big line with his right hand and arm, he pulled the dolphin in with his left hand. Its jaws were working hard in quick bites and it pounded the bottom of the boat with its long flat body. He hit it across the shining golden head until it shivered and was still.

The old man let go of the fish, added another sardine to the line and tossed it into the water. He worked his way slowly back to the bow. He washed his left hand and wiped it on his pants. Then he shifted the heavy line from his right hand to his left, and washed his right hand in the sea while he watched the sun set.

"He hasn't changed at all," he said. But watching the movement of the water against his hand he noted that it was much slower.

"I'll tie the two oars together across the stern, and that will slow him in the night," he said. "He's good for the night, and so am I."

It would be better to clean and cut the dolphin a little later to save the blood in the meat, he thought. I had better keep the fish quiet now and not disturb him too much at sunset. The setting of the sun is a difficult time for all fish.

Tomorrow I will eat the dolphin. Perhaps I should eat some of it when I clean it. It will be harder to eat than the tuna. But, then, nothing is easy.

"How do you feel, fish?" he asked aloud. "I feel good and my left hand is better and I have food for a night and a day. Pull the boat, fish."

It becomes dark quickly after the sun sets in September. He lay against the worn wood of the bow and rested as much as he could. The first stars were out.

He was sorry for the great fish that had

nothing to eat, but he still wanted to kill him. How many people will he feed, he thought. But are they worthy to eat him? No, of course not.

Now I will rest an hour more before I move back to the stern. In the meantime I can see how he acts and if he shows any changes. The punishment of his hunger and his fight with me, a human, is everything. Rest now, old man, and let the fish work until your next duty comes.

He rested for what he believed to be two hours.

"But you have not slept yet, old man," he said aloud. "It is half a day and a night and now another day and you have not slept. You must devise a way so that you sleep a little if he is quiet. If you do not sleep you might become unclear in the head."

My mind is clear, he thought. Maybe it is too clear. I am as clear as the stars that are my brothers. Still I must sleep. They sleep, and the moon and the sun sleep, and even the ocean sleeps sometimes on days when there is no current.

I could go without sleeping, he told himself. But it would be too dangerous.

He started to work his way to the back of the boat on his hands and knees, being careful not make any movement that the fish would feel. He may be half asleep, he thought. But I do not want him to rest. He must pull until he dies.

In the back of the boat, he turned so that his left hand held the line across his shoulders and drew his knife. The stars were bright now and he saw the dolphin clearly. He pushed the blade of his knife into its head. He put one of his feet on the fish and slit him quickly. Then he put his knife down and cleaned the guts.

He slid the dolphin carcass overboard and looked to see if there was any movement in the water. But there was only the light of its slow descent.

Back in the bow he laid the two pieces of flying fish from the dolphin's belly out on the wood. Then he washed the flying fish in the water, feeling the speed of the water against his hand.

"He is tired or he is resting," the old man said. "Now let me eat this dolphin and get some rest and a little sleep."

Under the stars and with the night colder all the time, he ate half of one of the dolphin pieces and one of the flying fish.

"What an excellent fish dolphin is to eat cooked," he said. "And what a terrible fish it is to eat raw."

But I have chewed it all well and I am not sick.

"There will be bad weather in three or four days," he said. "But not tonight and not tomorrow. Right now, you should get some sleep, old man, while the fish is quiet."

He held the line in his right hand and then pushed his thigh against his right hand, leaning all his weight against the wood of the bow. Then he passed the line a little lower on his shoulders and braced his left hand on it.

My right hand can hold on, he thought. If it relaxes in sleep my left hand will wake me as the line goes out. It is hard on the right hand. But he is used to punishment. Even if I sleep twenty minutes or half an hour, it is good. He lay forward, pushing himself against the line with all of his body, putting all of his weight on his right hand, and he fell asleep.

He did not dream about the lions of Africa, which was his usual dream. This time he dreamed about a school of porpoises. They were mating, and they would leap high into the air and return into the same hole they had made in the water.

Then he dreamed that he was in the village on his bed and there was a north wind. He was very cold, and his right arm was asleep because his head had rested on it instead of a pillow.

After that he began to dream about a long yellow beach in Africa, and he saw the first of the lions come down to it in the early dark.

The moon had been up for a long time, but he slept, and the fish pulled on.

He woke with the feeling of his right fist coming up against his face and the line burning out through his right hand. The line rushed out. Finally his left hand found the line. It burned his back and his left hand was taking all the line and getting cut badly. He looked back at the coils of line and they were moving.

Just then the fish jumped, making a great bursting out of the ocean and then a heavy fall. Then he jumped again and again and the boat was going fast although line was still racing out, and the old man was raising the line to the breaking point again and again. He had been pulled down on the bow. His face was pressed into the cut slice of dolphin meat and he could not move.

This is what we waited for, he thought. So now let us take it.

Make him pay for the line, he thought. Make him pay for it.

He could not see the fish's jumps, but he heard the breaking of the ocean and the heavy splash as the fish fell. The speed of the line was cutting his hands badly, but he had always known this would happen and he tried not to let the line slip into the palm or cut his fingers.

If the boy were here he would wet the coils of line, he thought. Yes. If the boy were here.

The line went out and out and out but it was slowing now and he was making the fish earn each inch of it. Now he raised his head up from the wood and out of the slice of fish that his cheek had crushed. He was on his knees and rose slowly to his feet. He could feel with his foot the coils of line that he could not see. There was a lot of line still and now the fish had to pull the friction of all that new line through the water.

Yes, he thought. Now he has jumped more than a dozen times and filled the sacks along his back with air and he cannot go down deep to die where I cannot bring him up. He will start circling soon and then I must work on him. I wonder what excited him so suddenly? Could it have been hunger that made him desperate, or was he frightened by something in the night? Maybe he suddenly felt fear. But he was such a strong fish and he seemed so confident. It is strange.

"You better be fearless and confident yourself, old man," he said.

The old man held him with his left hand and his shoulders now, and stooped down and scooped up water in his right hand to wash the crushed dolphin flesh off his face. When his face was cleaned he washed his right hand in the water over the side, and then let it stay in the salt water while he watched the first light come before the sunrise. He's headed almost east, he thought. That means he is tired and going with the current. Soon he will have to circle. Then our true work begins.

After he judged that his right hand had been in the water long enough he took it out and looked at it. "It is not bad," he said. "And pain does not matter to a man."

He took hold of the line carefully and shifted his weight so that he could put his left hand into the sea on the other side of the boat.

"You did not do so badly for something worthless," he said to his left hand. "But there was a moment when I could not find you."

Why was I not born with two good hands? he thought.

When he thought that he knew that he was not being clear-headed, he thought he should chew some more of the dolphin. But I can't, he told himself. It is better to be light-headed than to lose your strength from sickness. I will keep it for an emergency until it goes bad.

It is too late to try for strength now through nourishment. You're stupid, he told himself. Eat the other flying fish.

It was there, cleaned and ready, and he picked it up with his left hand and ate it, chewing the bones carefully and eating all of it down to the tail.

It has more nourishment than almost any fish, he thought, at least the kind of strength that I need. Now I have done what I can, he thought. Let him begin to circle and let the fight come.

The sun was rising for the third time since he had gone to sea when the fish started to circle.

He could not see by the slant of the line that the fish was circling. It was too early for that. He just felt less pressure on the line and he began to pull on it gently with his right hand. It tightened, as always, but just when he reached the point where it would break, the line began to come in. He slipped his shoulders and head from under the line and began to pull it in gently. He used both of his hands and tried to do the pulling as much as he could with his body and his legs.

"It is a very big circle," he said. "But he is circling."

Then the line would not come in any more, and he held it until he saw the drops jumping from it in the sun. Then it started out and the old man knelt down and let it go back into the dark water.

"He is making the far part of his circle now," he said. I must hold all I can, he thought. The line will shorten his circle each time. Perhaps in an hour I will see him. Now I must convince him, and then I must kill him.

But the fish kept on circling slowly, and the old man was wet with sweat and tired deep into his bones two hours later. But the circles were much shorter now, and from the way the line slanted he could tell the fish had risen while he swam.

For an hour the old man had been seeing black spots before his eyes, and the sweat salted his eyes and the cut over his eye on his head. He was not afraid of the black spots. They were normal with the tension that came from pulling on the line. Twice, though, he had felt dizzy, and that had worried him.

"I could not fail myself and die on a fish like this," he said. "Now that I have him coming so beautifully, God help me."

Just then he felt a sudden banging and jerking on the line he held with his two hands. It was sharp and hard and heavy.

He is hitting the leader with his spear, he thought. That was bound to come. He had to do that. It may make him jump, though, and I would rather he stayed circling now. The jumps were necessary for him to breathe air. But after that, each one can widen the opening of the wound.

"Don't jump, fish," he said.

The fish hit the line several times more, and each time he shook his head the old man released a little line.

I must hold his pain where it is, he thought. Mine does not matter. I can control mine. But his pain could drive him mad.

After a while, the fish stopped beating at the line and started circling slowly again. The old man felt dizzy again. He lifted some seawater with his left hand and put it on his head. Then he put more on and rubbed the back of his neck.

"I have no cramps," he said. "He'll be up soon and I can last. I have to last."

He kneeled against the bow and, for a moment, slipped the line over his back again.

I'm more tired than I have ever been, he thought, and now the wind is rising. But that will be good to take him in with. I need that badly.

His straw hat was far on the back of his head

and he sank down into the bow with the pull of the line as he felt the fish turn.

The sea had risen considerably. But it was a fair-weather breeze and he had to have it to get home.

"I'll just steer south and west," he said. "A man is never lost at sea and it is a long island."

It was on the third turn that he saw the fish first.

He saw him first as a dark shadow. It took so long to pass under the boat that he could not believe its length.

"No," he said. "He can't be that big."

But he was that big, and at the end of this circle he came to the surface only thirty yards away. The man saw his tail out of water. It was higher than a big blade. As the fish swam just below the surface, the old man could see his huge body and the purple stripes that banded him.

On this circle the old man could see the

fish's eye and the two gray sucking fish that swam around him. Sometimes they attached themselves to him. Sometimes they darted off.

The old man was sweating now, but not from the sun. On each turn the fish made he was gaining line, and the man was sure that in two turns more he would have a chance to get the harpoon in.

But I must get him closer, he thought. I mustn't try for the head. I must get the heart.

"Be strong, old man," he said.

On the next circle the fish's back was out but he was a little too far from the boat. On the next circle he was still too far away, but he was higher out of water and the old man was sure that by gaining some more line he could have him alongside the boat.

The fish was coming in on his circle now and only his great tail was moving. The old man pulled on him to bring him closer. For just a moment the fish turned a little on his side. Then he straightened himself and began another circle.

"I moved him," the old man said.

He felt weak again now but he held on to the great fish as hard as he could. I moved him, he thought. Maybe this time I can get him over. Pull, hands, he thought. Hold up, legs. Last for me, head. This time I'll pull him over.

But when he pulled with all his strength, the fish pulled and then righted himself and swam away.

"Fish," the old man said. "Fish, you are going to have to die. Do you have to kill me too?"

His mouth was too dry to speak but he could not reach for the water now. I must get him alongside the boat this time, he thought. I am not good for many more turns. Yes you are, he told himself. You're good forever.

On the next turn, he nearly had him. But again the fish righted himself and swam slowly away.

You are killing me, fish, the old man thought. But you have a right to. Never have I seen a greater, or more beautiful thing than you, brother. Come on and kill me. I do not care who kills who.

Now you are getting confused in the head, he thought. You must keep your head clear. Keep your head clear and know how to suffer like a man. Or a fish, he thought.

"Clear up, head," he said in a voice he could hardly hear. "Clear up."

I will try it once more.

He tried it once more and he felt himself going when he turned the fish. The fish righted himself and swam off again slowly, with its great tail weaving in the air.

He tried it again and it was the same. So, he thought, I will try it once again.

He took all his pain and what was left of his strength and his pride and he put it against the fish's agony, and the fish came over on his side and swam gently on his side, his bill almost touching the planking of the boat, and started to pass the boat, long, deep, wide, silver and barred with purple in the water.

The old man dropped the line and put his foot on it and lifted the harpoon as high as he could and drove it down with all his strength into the fish's side behind the great chest fin that rose high in the air. He felt the iron go in and he pushed on it and drove it further, and then pushed with all his weight.

Then the fish came alive, with his death in him, and rose high out of the water, showing all his great length and width and all his power and his beauty. He seemed to hang in the air above the old man in the boat. Then he fell into the water with a crash that sent spray over the old man and over all of the boat.

The old man felt sick, and he could not see well. But he cleared the harpoon line and let it run slowly through his hands and, when he

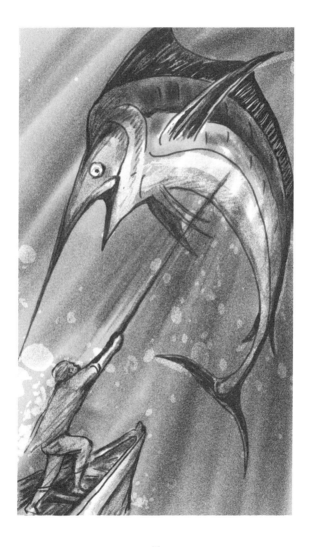

could see, he saw the fish was on his back with his silver belly up. The shaft of the harpoon was projecting at an angle from the fish's shoulder and the sea was red with the blood from his heart. First it was dark in the blue water that was more than a mile deep. Then it spread like a cloud. The fish was silvery and still and floated with the waves.

"Keep my head clear," the old man said against the wood of the bow. "I am a tired old man. But I have killed this fish which is my brother and now I must do the slave work."

Now I must prepare the nooses and the line to tie him to the boat, he thought. I must prepare everything and set sail for home.

He started to pull the fish in to have him alongside so that he could pass a line through his gills and out his mouth, and tie his head alongside the bow. I want to see him, he thought, and to touch and to feel him. He is my fortune, he thought. But that is not why I wish to feel him. I think I felt his heart, he thought.

"Get to work, old man," he said. He took a very small drink of the water. "There is very much work to be done now that the fight is over."

He looked up at the sky and then out to his fish. He looked at the sun carefully. It is not much more than noon, he thought.

"Come on, fish," he said. But the fish did not come. Instead he lay there in the seas and the old man pulled the boat up to him.

When he had the fish's head against the bow, he could not believe its size. But he untied the harpoon line, passed it through the fish's gills and out his jaws, made a turn around his sword then passed the line through the other gill. He cut the line then and went to the back of the boat to tie the tail. The fish had turned silver from his original purple and silver, and the stripes showed the same pale violet color as his tail.

"It was the only way to kill him," the old man said. He was feeling better and he knew he would not go away and his head was clear. The fish is over fifteen hundred pounds the way he is, he thought.

The boat began to move, and half lying in the stern, he sailed southwest.

He caught a patch of yellow seaweed with the gaff as he passed and shook it so that the small shrimps that were in it fell on the planking of the boat. There were more than a dozen of them and they jumped and kicked like sand fleas. The old man pinched their heads off with his thumb and forefinger and ate them chewing up the shells and the tails. They were very tiny but he knew they were nourishing and they tasted good.

The old man still had two drinks of water in the bottle and he used half of one after he had eaten the shrimps. The boat was sailing well. He could see the fish, he had only to look at his hands and feel his back against the stern to know that this had truly happened and was not a dream. At one time he had thought perhaps it was a dream. Then when he had seen the fish come out of the water and hang motionless in the sky before it fell, he was sure there was some great strangeness and he could not believe it.

Now he knew there was the fish. The hands cure quickly, he thought. I bled them clean and the salt water will heal them. The dark water of the sea is the greatest healer that there is. All I must do is keep my head clear. The hands have done their work and we sail well. With his mouth shut and his tail straight up, we sail like brothers.

Then his head started to become a little unclear and he thought, is he bringing me in or am I bringing him in? If I were towing him behind there would be no question. If the fish were in the boat, there would be no question either. But they were sailing together lashed side by side and the old man thought, let him bring me in if it pleases him. I am only better than him through my tricks, and he meant me no harm.

They sailed well and the old man soaked his hands in the salt water and tried to keep his head clear. The man looked at the fish constantly to make sure it was true.

It was an hour before the first shark hit him.

The shark was not an accident. He had come up from deep down in the water as the dark cloud of blood had settled and spread in the mile deep sea. He had come up so fast and without caution that he broke the surface of the blue water and was in the sun. Then he fell back into the sea and picked up the scent and started swimming on the course the boat and the fish had taken.

Sometimes the shark lost the scent. But he would pick it up again, or have just a trace of it, and he swam fast and hard on the course. He was a very big Mako shark, built to swim as fast as the fastest fish in the sea, and everything about him was beautiful except his jaws.

His back was as blue as a swordfish's and his belly was silver and his hide was smooth and handsome. He was built as a swordfish except for his huge jaws, which were shut now as he swam fast, just under the surface with his high dorsal fin knifing through the water. Inside the closed double lip of his jaws all of his eight rows of teeth were slanted inward.

They were not the ordinary pyramid-shaped teeth of most sharks. They were shaped like a man's finger, like claws. They were nearly as long as the fingers of the old man and they had razor-sharp cutting edges on both sides. Now he speeded up as he smelled the fresher scent and his blue dorsal fin cut the water.

When the old man saw him coming he knew that this was a shark that had no fear at all and would do exactly what he wished. He prepared the harpoon while he watched the shark come.

The old man's head was clear and good now and he was full of resolution, but he had little hope. It was too good to last, he thought. He took one look at the great fish as he watched the shark close in. It might as well have been a dream, he thought.

When the shark hit the fish the old man saw his mouth open, and his strange eyes and the clicking chop of the teeth as he drove forward in the meat just above the tail. The shark's head was out of water and his back was coming out and the old man could hear the noise of skin and flesh ripping on the big fish. He brought the harpoon down on the shark's head between his eyes. That was the location of the brain and the old man hit it. He hit it with all his strength.

The shark swung on its side and the old man saw his eye was not alive. The old man knew that he was dead but the shark would not accept it. Then, on his back, with his tail lashing and his jaws clicking, the shark swam fast over the water like a speedboat. The water was white where his tail beat it and three-quarters of his body was clear above the water when the line snapped. The shark lay quietly for a little while on the surface, and the old man watched him. Then he sank down very slowly.

He took my harpoon and all the line, he thought, and now my fish bleeds and there will be other sharks.

He did not like to look at the fish anymore since it had been mutilated. When the fish had been hit, the old man felt as though he himself were hit.

But I killed the shark that hit my fish, he thought.

It was too good to last, he thought. I wish it had been a dream now, and that I had never caught the fish and was alone in bed on the newspapers.

"But man is not made for defeat," he said. "A man can be destroyed but not defeated." I am sorry that I killed the fish, though, he thought. Now the bad time is coming and I do not even have the harpoon.

"Don't think, old man," he said aloud.

But I must think, he thought. Because it is all I have left.

"Think about something cheerful, old man," he said. "Every minute now you are closer to home."

He knew quite well what could happen when he reached the inner part of the current. But there was nothing to be done now.

"Yes there is," he said aloud. "I can lash my knife to the butt of one of the oars."

So he did that with the tiller under his arm and the sheet of the sail under his foot.

"Now," he said. "I am still an old man. But I am not unarmed."

The breeze was fresh now and he sailed on well. He watched only the front part of the fish and some of his hope returned.

It is silly not to hope, he thought. I believe it is a sin. Do not think about sin, he thought. There are enough problems now without sin. Also I have no understanding of it.

Perhaps it was a sin to kill the fish. I suppose it was even though I did it to keep me alive and feed many people. But then everything is a sin. Do not think about sin. It is much too late for that and there are people who are paid to do it. Let them think about it. You were born to be a fisherman as the fish was born to be a fish.

But he liked to think about all things that he was involved in and since there was nothing to read and he did not have a radio, he thought much and kept on thinking about sin. You did not kill the fish only to keep alive and to sell for food, he thought. You killed him for pride, and because you are a fisherman. You loved him when he was alive and you loved him after. If you love him, it is not a sin to kill him. Or is it more?

"You think too much, old man," he said aloud.

Everything kills everything else in some way, he thought. Fishing kills me exactly as it keeps me alive. The boy keeps me alive, he thought. I must not deceive myself too much.

He pulled loose a piece of the meat of the fish where the shark had cut him. He chewed it and noted its quality and its good taste. It was firm and juicy, like meat, but it was not red. It was also tender, and he knew it would bring the highest price in the market. But there was no way to keep this scent out of the water and the old man knew that a very bad time was coming.

He had sailed for two hours, resting in the stern and sometimes chewing a bit of the meat from the marlin, trying to rest and to be strong, when he saw the first of the two sharks.

"*Ay*," he said aloud.

He had seen the second fin now coming up behind the first, and had identified them as shovel-nosed sharks by the brown, triangular fin and the sweeping movements of the tail. They had smelled his fish and were excited.

The old man took up the oar with the knife lashed to it. He lifted it as lightly as he could because his hands hurt. He closed them firmly so they would take the pain now and watched the sharks come. He could see their wide, flattened, shovel-pointed heads now and their white-tipped wide fins. They were hateful sharks, bad smelling, scavengers as well as killers, and when they were hungry they would bite at an oar or the rudder of a boat.

They came. But they did not come as the Mako sharks had come. One turned and went out of sight under the boat, and the old man could feel the boat shake as it jerked and pulled on the fish. The other watched the old man with his slitted yellow eyes, and then came in fast with his jaws wide to hit the fish where he had already been bitten. The old man drove the knife on the oar into the shark's head, withdrew it, and drove it in again. The shark let go of the fish and slid down, swallowing what he had taken as he died.

The boat was still shaking from the other shark. When the old man saw the shark he punched at him. He hit only meat, and the hide was hard and he barely got the knife in. The blow hurt not only his hands but his shoulder too. But the shark came up fast with his head out and the old man hit him squarely in the center of his flat-topped head, as his nose came out of the water and lay against the fish. The old man withdrew the blade and punched the shark in the same spot again. He still hung on to the fish with his jaws caught and the old man stabbed him in his left eye. The shark still hung there.

"No?" the old man said, and he drove the blade between the back and the brain. The old man reversed the oar and put the blade between the shark's jaws to open them. He twisted the blade, and as the shark slid loose he said, "Go on. Slide down a mile deep. Go see your friend, or maybe it's your mother."

The old man wiped the blade of his knife and laid down the oar. Then he brought the boat on course.

"They must have taken a quarter of my fish," he said aloud. "I wish it were a dream and that I had never caught him. I'm sorry about it, fish. It makes everything wrong." He stopped and he did not want to look at the fish now.

"I shouldn't have sailed out so far, fish," he said. "Neither for you nor for me. I'm sorry, fish."

Now, he said to himself, get your hand in order because there still is more to come.

"I wish I had a stone to sharpen the knife,"

the old man said. "I should have brought a stone." You should have brought many things, he thought. But you did not bring them, old man. Now is no time to think of what you do not have. Think of what you can do with what there is.

"You give me much good advice," he said to himself. "I'm tired of it."

He soaked both his hands in the water as the boat drove forward.

The next shark that came was a single shovel-nose. The old man let him hit the fish, and then drove the knife on the oar down into his brain. But the shark jerked backwards and the knife blade snapped.

The old man settled himself to steer. He did not even watch the big shark sinking slowly in the water, showing first life-size, then small, then tiny. That always interested the old man. But he did not even watch it now.

Now they have beaten me, he thought. I am

too old to club sharks to death. But I will try it as long as I have the oars and the short club and the tiller.

He put his hands in the water again to soak them. It was getting late in the afternoon and he saw nothing but the sea and the sky. He hoped that he would soon see land.

"You're tired, old man," he said.

The sharks did not hit him again until just before sunset.

The old man saw the brown fins coming. They were headed straight for the boat, swimming side by side.

He reached under the stern for the club. It was an oar handle from a broken oar sawed off to about two and a half feet in length. He could only use it effectively with one hand because of the grip of the handle, and he took hold of it with his right hand as he watched the sharks come.

I must let the first one get a good hold on

my fish and hit him on the point of the nose, or straight across the top of the head, he thought.

The two sharks came closer and as the one nearest opened his jaws, he raised the club high and brought it down heavy, slamming on the top of the shark's broad head.

The other shark had been in and out and now came in again with his jaws wide. The old man swung at him and hit only the head, and the shark looked at him and pulled the meat loose. The old man swung the club down on him again as he slipped away.

The shark came in a rush and the old man hit him as he shut his jaws. The old man watched for him to come again but neither shark showed. Then he saw one on the surface swimming in circles. He did not see the fin of the other.

I could not expect to kill them, he thought. But I have hurt them both badly and neither one can feel very good.

He did not want to look at the fish. He knew that half of him had been destroyed. The sun had gone down while he had been in the fight with the sharks.

"It will be dark soon," he said. "Then I should see the glow of Havana."

I cannot be too far out now, he thought. I hope no one has been too worried. There is only the boy to worry, of course. But I am sure he would have confidence. Many of the older fishermen will worry. Many others too, he thought. I live in a good town.

He could not talk to the fish anymore because the fish had been ruined. Then something came into his head.

"Half fish," he said. "Fish that you were. I am sorry that I went too far out. I ruined us both. But we have killed many sharks, you and I, and ruined many others. How many did you ever kill, old fish? You do not have that spear on your head for nothing."

In the dark now, he felt that perhaps he was already dead. He put his two hands together and felt the palms. They were not dead and he could bring the pain of life by simply opening and closing them. He pushed his back against the stern and knew he was not dead. His shoulders told him.

He lay in the stern and steered and watched for the glow to come in the sky. I have half of my fish, he thought. Maybe I'll have the luck to bring the forward half in.

I must not think nonsense, he thought. Luck is a thing that comes in many forms and who can recognize her?

He saw the reflected glare of the lights of the city at what must have been around ten o'clock at night. Now it is over, he thought. The sharks will probably hit me again. But what can a man do against them in the dark without a weapon?

He was stiff and sore and his wounds and all of the parts of his body hurt with the cold of the night. I hope I do not have to fight again, he thought.

But by midnight he fought, and this time he knew the fight was useless. The sharks came in a group. He clubbed at heads and heard the jaws chop and the shaking of the boat. He clubbed at what he could only feel and hear, and he felt something steal his club and it was gone.

The sharks were tearing off the pieces of meat.

One came, finally, to eat the head of his fish. That was the last shark of the pack that came. There was nothing more for them to eat.

The old man could hardly breathe now and he felt a strange taste in his mouth. He spat into the ocean.

He knew he was beaten now, finally, and nothing would change that. He could see the lights of the beach colonies along the shore. He knew where he was now and it would be easy to get home.

The wind is my friend, anyway, he thought. And bed, he thought. Bed is my friend. It is easy when you are beaten, he thought. I never knew how easy it was. And what beat you, he thought.

"Nothing," he said aloud. "I went out too far."

When he sailed into the little harbor the lights of the Terrace were out and he knew everyone was in bed. There was no one to help him so he pulled the boat up as far as he could.

He stopped for a moment and looked back and saw in the reflection from the street light the great tail of the fish standing up behind the boat's stern.

He started to climb again and he fell and lay for some time with the mast across his shoulder. He tried to get up. But it was too difficult and he sat there with the mast on his shoulder and looked at the road.

He had to sit down five times before he reached his shack.

Inside the shack he put the mast against the wall. In the dark he found a water bottle and took a drink. Then he lay down on the bed. He pulled the blanket over his shoulders and he slept face down on the newspapers with his arms out straight and the palms of his hands up.

He was asleep when the boy looked in the door in the morning. The boy saw that the old man was breathing and then he saw the old man's hands and he started to cry. He went out very quietly to go to bring some coffee and all the way down the road he was crying.

Many fishermen were around the boat. One was in the water, his pants rolled up, measuring the fish skeleton with a length of line.

"How is he?" one of the fishermen shouted to the boy.

"Sleeping," the boy called. He did not care that they saw him crying. "Let no one disturb him."

"The fish was eighteen feet from nose to tail."

"I believe it," the boy said.

He went into the Terrace and asked for a can of coffee.

"What a fish it was," the proprietor said. "There has never been such a fish. Those were two fine fish you took yesterday too."

The boy carried the hot can of coffee up to the old man's shack and sat by him until he woke.

"Don't sit up," the boy said. "Drink this." He poured some of the coffee in a glass.

The old man took it and drank it.

"They beat me, Manolin," he said. "They truly beat me."

"He didn't beat you. Not the fish."

"No. Truly. It was afterwards. Did they search for me?"

"Of course. With coast guard and with planes."

"The ocean is very big and a boat is small

and hard to see," the old man said. He noticed how pleasant it was to have someone to talk to instead of speaking only to himself and to the sea. "I missed you," he said.

"Now we fish together again."

"No. I am not lucky. I am not lucky anymore."

"The hell with luck," the boy said. "I'll bring the luck with me."

"What will your family say?"

"I do not care. We will fish together now for I still have much to learn. You must get well fast for there is much that I can learn and you can teach me everything. How much did you suffer?"

"A lot," the old man said.

"I'll bring the food and the papers," the boy said. "Rest well, old man. I will bring stuff from the drug-store for your hands."

As the boy went out the door and down the worn coral rock road, he was crying again.

That afternoon there was a party of tourists at the Terrace. Looking down in the water among the empty beer cans and dead barracudas, a woman saw a great long white spine with a huge tail.

"What's that?" she asked a waiter, and pointed to the long backbone of the great fish that was now just garbage waiting to go out with the tide.

"Tiburon," the waiter said, "Eshark." He was meaning to explain what had happened.

"I didn't know sharks had such handsome, beautifully formed tails."

"I didn't either," her male companion said.

Up the road, in his shack, the old man was sleeping again. He was still sleeping on his face and the boy was sitting by him watching him. The old man was dreaming about the lions in Africa.

Word List

A

□ **accept** 動 ①受け入れる ②同意する, 認める

□ **accident** 名 ①(不慮の) 事故, 災難 ②偶然

□ **act** 動 ①行動する ②演じる

□ **add** 動 加える, 足す

□ **advice** 名 忠告, 助言, 意見

□ **afraid of** 《be -》~を恐れる, ~を怖がる

□ **Africa** 名 アフリカ《大陸》

□ **after a while** しばらくして

□ **after that** その後

□ **afterwards** 副 その後, のちに

□ **again and again** 何度も繰り返して

□ **against** 熟 against the wall 壁を背にして come up against ~にぶつかる push against ~で…を押す

□ **agony** 名 苦悩, 激しい苦痛

□ **ahead of** ・ より先[前]に, ~に先んじて

□ **aid** 名 援助 (者), 助け come to someone's aid (人) の救助に向かう

□ **albacore** 名 ビンナガ《魚》

□ **all** 熟 all day 一日中, 明けても暮れても all over ~中で, 全体に亘って, ~の至る所で all the time ずっと, いつも, その間ずっと all the way ずっと, はるばる, いろいろと at all とにかく not ~ at all 少しも [全然] ~ない over all 全体にわたって

□ **alongside** 副 そばに, 並んで 前 ~のそばに, ~と並んで

□ **aloud** 副 大声で, (聞こえるように) 声を出して

□ **although** 接 ~だけれども, ~にもかかわらず, たとえ~でも

□ **always** 熟 as always いつものように

□ **and so** そこで, それだから, それで

□ **angle** 名 ①角度 ②角

□ **another** 熟 one another お互い

□ **any** 熟 not ~ any more もう [これ以上] ~ない

□ **anymore** 副 《通例否定文, 疑問文で》今はもう, これ以上, これから

□ **anyone** 代 ①《疑問文・条件節で》誰か ②《否定文で》誰も (~ない) ③《肯定文で》誰でも

□ **anyway** 副 ①いずれにせよ, ともかく ②どんな方法でも

74

□ **around** 熟 turn around 振り向く, 向きを変える, 方向転換する

□ **as** 熟 as always いつものように as far as ～と同じくらい遠く, ～まで, ～する限り(では) as far as one can できるだけ as long as ～する以上は, ～である限りは as much as ～と同じだけ as though あたかも～のように, まるで～みたいで as well なお, その上, 同様に as well as ～と同様に as ～ as one can できる限り～ see ～ as … ～を…と考える such as たとえば～, ～のような the same ～ as … …と同じ(ような)～

□ **asleep** 形 ①眠って(いる状態の) ②無感覚で, しびれて fall asleep 眠り込む, 寝入る

□ **at least** 少なくとも

□ **at one time** ある時には, かつては

□ **at the end of** ～の終わりに

□ **at this** これを見て, そこで(すぐに)

□ **attach** 動 ①取り付ける, 添える ②付随する, 帰属する

□ **attention** 名 注意, 集中 pay attention to ～に注意を払う

□ **away** 熟 far away 遠く離れて fly away 飛び去る go away 立ち去る move away 立ち去る slip away すり抜ける, こっそり去る, 静かに立ち去る

□ **Ay** 間 おお, ああ《悲哀, 後悔・驚きなどを表す叫び》

□ **back** 熟 fall back 後退する, 戻る, 退却する look back at ～に視線を戻す, ～を振り返って見る push back 押し返す, 押しのける

B

□ **backbone** 名 背骨

□ **backwards** 副 後方へ, 逆に, 後ろ向きに

□ **badly** 副 悪く, まずく, へたに

□ **bait** 名 えさ

□ **band** 動 ひもで縛る

□ **bang** 動 ドスンと鳴る, 強く打つ

□ **banging** 名 激しく打つこと, 絶え間ない大騒音

□ **Bare-footed** 形 はだしの

□ **barely** 副 ①かろうじて, やっと ②ほぼ, もう少しで

□ **barracuda** 名 バラクーダ《魚》

□ **barred** 形 縞のある

□ **baseball** 名 野球

□ **beat** 動 ①打つ, 鼓動する ②打ち負かす

□ **beaten** 動 beat (打つ) の過去分詞 形 打たれた, 打ち負かされた, 疲れ切った

□ **beating** 打つこと, たたくこと

□ **beautifully** 副 美しく, 立派に, 見事に

□ **beauty** 名 美, 美しい人[物]

□ **because of** ～のために, ～の理由で

□ **beer** 名 ビール

□ **behind** 前 ～の後ろに, ～の背後に 副 後ろに, 背後に

□ **belly** 名 腹

□ **below** 前 ～より下に

□ **better** 熟 feel better 気分がよくなる get better (病気などが) 良くなる had better ～したほうが身のためだ, ～しなさい

□ **bill** 名 くちばし

□ **bit** 名《a-》少し, ちょっと

□ **bite** 動 かむ, かじる 名 かむこと, かみ傷, ひと口

□ **bitten** 動 bite (かむ) の過去分詞

□ **blade** 名 ①(刀・ナイフなどの) 刃 ②(オールの) 水かき, ブレード

□ **blanket** 名 毛布

□ **bled** 動 bleed（出血する）の過去, 過去分詞

□ **bleed** 動 出血する, 血を流す［流させる］

□ **blood** 名 血, 血液

□ **bloody** 形 血だらけの

□ **blow** （風が）吹く,（風が）～を吹き飛ばす 名（風の）ひと吹き, 突風

□ **bone** 名 骨,《-s》骨格 **back bone** 背骨

□ **both A and B** AもBも

□ **bottom** 名 底, 下部

□ **bound** 動 bind（縛る）の過去, 過去分詞 **be bound to** きっと～する, ～する義務がある

□ **bow** 名 船首

□ **boy** 熟 **my boy** 息子

□ **brace** 動 ①元気づける ②気を引き締める ③支える

□ **brain** 名 脳

□ **breaking** 名 破壊

□ **breaking point** 限界点

□ **breathe** 動 呼吸する

□ **breeze** 名 そよ風

□ **bring down** 打ち降ろす

□ **bring in** 持ち込む

□ **bring up** 連れて行く

□ **broad** 形 幅の広い

□ **burn out** 焼き切る

□ **bursting** 名 破裂

□ **but** 熟 **not only ～ but …** ～だけでなく…もまた **not ～ but …** ～ではなくて… **nothing but** ただ～だけ, ～にすぎない, ～のほかは何も…ない

□ **butt** 名（武器・道具の）大きいほうの端

□ **by oneself** 一人で, 自分だけで, 独力で

C

□ **can** 熟 **Can I ～?** ～してもよいですか。 **Can you ～?** ～してくれますか。 **as far as one can** できるだけ **as ～ as one can** できる限り～ **can do nothing** どうしようもない **can hardly** とても～できない, かろうじて～できる

□ **cancer** 名 癌

□ **carcass** 名 残骸, 死骸

□ **carry on** 持ち運ぶ

□ **cast** 名 投げること **cast net** 投網

□ **caution** 名 用心, 注意, 警告

□ **check** 動 照合する, 検査する

□ **cheek** 名 ほお

□ **cheerful** 形 上機嫌の, 元気のよい,（人を）気持ちよくさせる

□ **chest** 名 胸, 肺

□ **chew** 動 かむ

□ **chin** 名 あご

□ **chop** 動 たたき切る, 切り刻む 名 一撃, チョップ

□ **circle** 名 ①円, 円周, 輪 ②循環, 軌道 動 回る, 囲む

□ **claw** 名 鉤爪

□ **clear** 形 ①はっきりした, 明白な ②澄んだ ③（よく）晴れた 動 ①はっきりさせる ②片づける ③晴れる **clear up** きれいにする, 片付ける,（疑問, 問題を）解決する 副 ①はっきりと ②すっかり, 完全に

□ **clear-headed** 形 頭のさえた, 意識がはっきりした

□ **clearly** 副 明らかに, はっきりと

□ **click** 動 ①カチッと音がする［音をさせる］ ②（ボタンを）カチッと押す, クリックする

□ **clicking** 形 カチッという音の

□ **closed** 動 close（閉まる）の過去, 過去分詞 形 閉じた, 閉鎖した

□ **coast** 名 海岸, 沿岸 **coast guard** 沿岸警備隊（員）

A
B
C
D
E
F
G
H
I
J
K
L
M
N
O
P
Q
R
S
T
U
V
W
X
Y
Z

□ **coil** 名 ぐるぐる巻いたもの, コイル

□ **coiled** 形 ひもなどでグルグル巻きにされた

□ **colony** 名〔同じ民族から構成される〕居留地

□ **come** 熟 come down 下りて来る come in 中にははいる, やってくる come into ～に入ってくる come on さあ来なさい come out 出てくる, 姿を現す come out of ～から出てくる come over やって来る come to someone's aid (人) の救助に向かう come up 近づいてくる, 浮上する, 水面へ上ってくる come up against ～にぶつかる

□ **companion** 名 友, 仲間, 連れ

□ **confidence** 名 自信, 確信, 信頼, 信用度

□ **confident** 形 自信のある, 自信に満ちた

□ **confused** 形 困惑した, 混乱した

□ **considerably** 副 かなり, 相当に

□ **constantly** 副 絶えず, いつも, 絶え間なく

□ **control** 動 ①管理 [支配] する ②抑制する, コントロールする

□ **convince** 動 納得させる, 確信させる

□ **coral** 名 サンゴ (珊瑚) 形 サンゴの

□ **could** 熟 If +《主語》+ could ～できればなあ《仮定法》could have done ～だったかもしれない《仮定法》

□ **course** 熟 of course もちろん, 当然

□ **cover** 動 覆う, 包む, 隠す

□ **cramp** 動 けいれんする

□ **crash** 名 ①激突, 墜落 ②(壊れるときの) すさまじい音

□ **cream** 名 クリーム

□ **credit** 名 掛け売り, 信用貸し

□ **crouch** 動 しゃがむ, うずくまる

□ **crush** 動 押しつぶす, 砕く, 粉々にする

□ **crushed** 形 押しつぶされた

□ **cure** 動 治療する, 矯正する

□ **current** 名 流れ

□ **cutting edge** 刃の先端, 刃先

D

□ **darkness** 名 暗さ, 暗やみ

□ **dart** 動 (矢, 視線などを) 投げる, 射る dart off 駆け去る

□ **day** 熟 all day 一日中, 明けても暮れても each day 毎日, 日ごとに every day 毎日 these days このごろ

□ **daylight** 名 夜明け

□ **death** 名 ①死, 死ぬこと ②《the-》終えん, 消滅 to death 死ぬまで, 死ぬほど

□ **deceive** 動 だます, あざむく

□ **defeat** 動 ①打ち破る, 負かす ②だめにする 名 ①敗北 ②挫折

□ **depth** 名 深さ, 奥行き, 深いところ

□ **descent** 名 下り坂, 下降

□ **desperate** 形 ①絶望的な, 見込みのない ②ほしくてたまらない, 必死の

□ **desperately** 副 絶望的に, 必死になって

□ **destroy** 動 破壊する, 絶滅させる, 無効にする

□ **devise** 動 工夫する, 考案する

□ **dip** 動 ちょっと浸す, さっとつける 名〔物を〕下げる [沈める・浸す] こと

□ **direction** 名 方向, 方角

□ **disturb** 動 かき乱す, 妨げる

□ **dizzy** 形 めまいがする, 目が回る, くらくらする

□ **dolphin** 名 シイラ《魚》

77

□ **don't have to** ～する必要はない

□ **done for** 《be～》死ぬ

□ **dorsal** 形背(面)の dorsal fin 背びれ

□ **double** 形 ①2倍の, 二重の ②対の

□ **doubt** 動疑う

□ **dove** 動dive (飛び込む) の過去

□ **down** 熟 bring down 打ち降ろす come down 下りて来る down to ～に至るまで face down ～に敢然と立ち向かう, 威圧する go down 下に降りる lay down 下に置く, 横たえる lie down 横たわる, 横になる look down 見下ろす put down 下に置く, 下ろす run down (液体が) 流れ落ちる, 駆け下りる take down 下げる, 降ろす up and down 上がったり下がったり, 行ったり来たり, あちこちと

□ **dozen** 名1ダース, 12(個)

□ **dream of** ～を夢見る

□ **drew** 動draw (引く) の過去

□ **drove** 動drive (車で行く) の過去

□ **drug-store** 名薬局

□ **duty** 名職務, 任務

E

□ **each day** 毎日, 日ごとに

□ **each one** 各自

□ **each time** ～するたびに

□ **earn** 動儲ける, 稼ぐ

□ **eastward** 形東 (へ) の, 東方 (へ) の

□ **edge** 名 ①刃 ②端, 縁 cutting edge 刃の先端, 刃先

□ **effectively** 副効果的に, 効率的に

□ **emergency** 名非常時, 緊急時

□ **end** 熟 at the end of ～の終わりに

□ **entire** 形全体の, 完全な, まったくの

□ **eshark** 俗サメ 《a shark が訛った音》

□ **even if** たとえ～でも

□ **even though** ～であるけれども, ～にもかかわらず

□ **every day** 毎日

□ **everyone** 代誰でも, 皆

□ **everything** 代すべてのこと [もの], 何でも, 何もかも

□ **exact** 形正確な, 厳密な, きちょうめんな

□ **excellent** 形優れた, 優秀な

□ **except** 前～を除いて, ～のほかは except for ～を除いて, ～がなければ

□ **excited** 動excite (興奮する) の過去, 過去分詞 形興奮した, わくわくした

□ **expect** 動予期 [予測] する, (当然のこととして) 期待する

F

□ **face down** ～に敢然と立ち向かう, 威圧する

□ **fail** 動 ①失敗する ②裏切る, 失望させる

□ **fair-weather** 形晴天のときだけの, 晴天向きの

□ **fall asleep** 眠り込む, 寝入る

□ **fall back** 後退する, 戻る, 退却する

□ **fall into** ～に陥る, ～してしまう

□ **far** 熟 as far as ～と同じくらい遠く, ～まで, ～する限り (では) as far as one can できるだけ遠く離れて far from ～から遠い, ～どころか far out はるか向こうに [で] go far 遠くへ行く so far 今までのところ, これまでは

☐ **favorable** 形 好意的な, 都合のよい

☐ **fear** 名 ①恐れ ②心配, 不安 **in fear** おどおどして, ビクビクして 動 ①恐れる ②心配する

☐ **fearless** 形 こわいもの知らずの, 大胆な

☐ **feed** 動 ①食物を与える ②供給する

☐ **feel better** 気分がよくなる

☐ **feel sick** 気分が悪い

☐ **feel sorry for** ~をかわいそうに思う

☐ **feeling** 動 feel (感じる) の現在分詞 名 感じ, 気持ち

☐ **feet** 熟 **rise to one's feet** 立ち上がる

☐ **fin** 名 (魚などの) ひれ, ひれ状のもの

☐ **firm** 形 堅い, しっかりした, 断固とした

☐ **firmly** 副 しっかりと, 断固として

☐ **first** 熟 **head first** 頭から真っ逆さまに

☐ **fisherman** 名 漁師, (趣味の) 釣り人

☐ **fishermen** 名 fisherman (漁師の複数形)

☐ **fishing** 動 fish (釣りをする) の現在分詞 名 釣り, 魚業 形 釣りの, 漁業の

☐ **fishing line** 釣り糸

☐ **fist** 名 こぶし, げんこつ

☐ **flat** 形 平らな

☐ **flat-topped** 形 上部が平たい, ぺったんこの

☐ **flattened** 形 扁平な, ぺちゃんこになった

☐ **flea** 名 ノミ (蚤)

☐ **flesh** 名 肉

☐ **float** 動 浮く, 浮かぶ

☐ **fly away** 飛び去る

☐ **flying fish** トビウオ《魚》

☐ **folded** 形 折り畳まれた

☐ **for a moment** 少しの間

☐ **for nothing** ただで, 無料で, むだに

☐ **for some time** しばらくの間

☐ **for years** 何年も

☐ **forefinger** 名 人差し指

☐ **forehead** 名 ひたい

☐ **form** 名 形, 形式 動 形づくる

☐ **fortune** 名 ①富, 財産 ②幸運, 繁栄, チャンス ③運命, 運勢

☐ **forward** 形 ①前方の, 前方へ向かう ②先の 副 ①前方に ②先へ, 進んで

☐ **friction** 名 摩擦, 不和

☐ **frightened** 形 おびえた, びっくりした

☐ **full of** 《be –》~で一杯である

☐ **full-blooded** 形 ①血がいっぱいつまった ②血気さかんな

☐ **fun** 熟 **make fun of** ~を物笑いの種にする, からかう

☐ **further** 副 いっそう遠く, その上に, もっと

G

☐ **gaff** 名 魚鉤 (かぎ), やす

☐ **gain** 動 ①得る, 増す ②進歩する, 進む

☐ **gamble** 動 賭ける, 賭け事をする

☐ **garbage** 名 ごみ, くず

☐ **gear** 名 用具, 装具

☐ **gentle** 形 ①優しい, 温和な ②柔らかな

☐ **gently** 副 親切に, 上品に, そっと, 優しく

☐ **get** 熟 **get better** (病気などが) 良く

なる **get home** 家に着く[帰る] **get into** 〜に入る, 入り込む, 〜に巻き込まれる **get over**〔困難・病気など〕克服する, 打ち勝つ **get someone to do** (人)に〜させる[してもらう] **get to** (事)を始める **get up** 起き上がる, 立ち上がる **get well** (病気が)よくなる

□ **gill** 名えら

□ **glare** 名ギラギラ光ること, まぶしい光

□ **glow** 名白熱, 輝き

□ **go** 熟 **go and** 〜しに行く **go away** 立ち去る **go down** 下に降りる **go far** 遠くへ行く **go in** 中に入る **go into** 〜に入る **Go on.** さあ行きなさい。 **go out** 外出する, 外へ出る・出ていく **go up** ①〜に上がる, 登る ②〜に近づく, 出かける **go with** 〜と一緒に行く, 〜と調和する **go without** 〜なしですませる **let go of** 〜を解き放つ

□ **golden** 形金色の

□ **good** 熟 **be not good for** 〜に良くない **do 〜 no good** 〜に効き目がない **too good to last** 良いことは長く続かない

□ **grab** 動①ふいにつかむ, ひったくる

□ **grip** 名つかむこと, 把握, グリップ

□ **group** 熟 **in a group** グループで

□ **guard** 名①警戒, 見張り ②番人 **coast guard** 沿岸警備隊(員)

□ **gut** 名腸, はらわた

H

□ **had better** 〜したほうが身のためだ, 〜しなさい

□ **handle** 名取っ手, 握り 動操縦する, 取り扱う

□ **handsome** 形端正な(顔立ちの), りっぱな

□ **hang** 動かかる, かける, つるす, ぶら下がる **hang on** 〜につかまる, しがみつく, がんばる

□ **harbor** 名港

□ **hard to** 〜し難い

□ **hardly** 副①ほとんど〜でない, わずかに ②厳しく, かろうじて **can hardly** とても〜できない, かろうじて〜できる

□ **harm** 名害, 損害, 危害

□ **harpoon** 名銛(もり)

□ **hate** 動嫌う, 憎む, (〜するのを)いやがる

□ **hateful** 形憎らしい, 忌まわしい

□ **Havana** 名ハバナ《キューバの首都》

□ **have** 熟 **could have done** 〜だったかもしれない《仮定法》 **don't have to** 〜する必要はない **should have done** 〜すべきだった(のにしなかった)《仮定法》 **will have done** 〜してしまっているだろう《未来完了形》 **would have … if** 〜もし〜だったとしたら…しただろう

□ **head first** 頭から真っ逆さまに

□ **head for** 〜に向かう, 〜の方に進む

□ **heal** 動いえる, いやす, 治る, 治す

□ **healer** 名薬, 治療する人

□ **held together with** 《be 〜》〜でとめられている[結び付けられている]

□ **hell** 名地獄, 地獄のようなところ[状態] **hell with** どうなっても構わない, まっぴらだ

□ **help 〜 to …** 〜が…するのを助ける

□ **hide** 名皮革, 〔けだものの〕皮

□ **hold** 熟 **hold on** しっかりつかまる **hold on to** 〜にしがみつく, 〜をつかんで放さない **hold up** ①維持する, 支える ②〜を持ち上げる ③(指を)立てる **hold with** 〜に賛成する

take hold of ～をつかむ, 捕らえる, 制する

☐ **home** 熟 get home 家に着く[帰る] take someone home ～を家へ持って帰る

☐ **hook** 名 止め金, 釣り針 動引っかける, 留める

☐ **how to** ～する方法

☐ **huge** 形巨大な, ばく大な

☐ **hung** 動 hang (かかる) の過去, 過去分詞

☐ **hunger** 名 空腹, 飢え 動飢える

☐ **hurricane** 名ハリケーン

I

☐ **icehouse** 名 氷室《ひむろ, 氷を常置してある貯蔵庫》

☐ **identify** 動 (本人・同一と) 確認する, 見分ける

☐ **if** 熟 If +《主語》+ could ～できればなあ《仮定法》 even if たとえ～でも see if ～かどうかを確かめる would have … if ～ もし～だったとしたら…しただろう

☐ **in** 熟 in a group グループで in fear おどおどして, ビクビクして in order きちんと (整理されて), 順序正しく in order to ～するために, ～しようと in some way 何とかして, 何らかの方法で in the meantime それまでは, 当分は

☐ **in order** きちんと (整理されて), 順序正しく

☐ **in order to** ～するために, ～しようと

☐ **inch** 名 ①インチ《長さの単位。1/12 フィート, 2.54cm》②少量

☐ **increase** 動増加[増強]する, 増やす, 増える

☐ **inner** 形 ①内部の ②心の中の

☐ **instead** 副 その代わりに instead of ～の代わりに, ～をしないで

☐ **involved in**《be –》〔活動など〕に従事[関与]している

☐ **inwards** 副内側 [内部・中心] へ

☐ **iron** 名鉄, 鉄製のもの

☐ **It is ～ for someone to …** (人) が…するのは～だ

J

☐ **jaw** 名 ①あご ②《-s》あご状のもの

☐ **jerk** 動急に動かす, ぐいと動く

☐ **judge** 動判断する, 評価する

☐ **juicy** 形 (汁・水分が) 多い

☐ **jump out of** ～から飛び出す

☐ **just then** そのとたんに

K

☐ **keep on -ing** ～し続ける, 繰り返し～する

☐ **keep up** 頑張り続ける, 持続する

☐ **killer** 名殺人者 [犯]

☐ **kind of** ～のようなもの [人]

☐ **knee** 名ひざ

☐ **kneel** 動ひざまずく, ひざをつく

☐ **knelt** 動 kneel (ひざまずく) の過去, 過去分詞

☐ **knife** 名ナイフ, 小刀, 包丁, 短剣

☐ **know** 熟 Who knows? 誰にわかるだろうか。誰にもわからない。

L

☐ **laid** 動 lay (置く) の過去, 過去分詞

☐ **lash** 動〔ひもやロープなどで～を〕固定する, 結び付ける

☐ **last** 熟 too good to last 良いことは長く続かない

□ **late for** 《be –》～に遅れる

□ **lavender** 形 ラベンダー色の, 薄紫色の

□ **lay** ①置く, 横たえる, 敷く ②lie (横たわる) の過去 **lay down** 下に置く, 横たえる

□ **leader** 名 [釣りの] はりす《釣り針を結んでいる短い釣り糸》

□ **lean** 動 ①もたれる, 寄りかかる ②傾く, 傾ける

□ **leap** 動 ①跳ぶ ②跳び越える

□ **least** 名 最小, 最少 **at least** 少なくとも

□ **leave** 熟 **make someone leave** 退職させる

□ **length** 名 長さ, 縦, たけ, 距離

□ **less** 副 ～より少なく, ～ほどでなく

□ **lesser** 形 小さいほうの, 劣ったほうの

□ **let go of** ～を解き放つ

□ **let us** どうか私たちに～させてください

□ **level** 名 [ある特定の] 高さ, 高度, 深さ

□ **lie down** 横たわる, 横になる

□ **life-size** 形 等身大の

□ **lift** 動 持ち上げる

□ **light-headed** 形 軽薄な

□ **lightly** 副 軽く, そっと

□ **like** 熟 **like this** このような, こんなふうに **look like** ～のように見える, ～に似ている **would like to** ～したいと思う

□ **lip** 名 唇

□ **location** 名 位置, 場所

□ **lonely** 形 孤独な, 心さびしい

□ **long** 熟 **as long as** ～する以上は, ～である限りは

□ **look** 熟 **look back at** ～に視線を戻す, ～を振り返って見る **look down** 見下ろす **look for** ～を探す **look in** 中を見る, 立ち寄る **look like** ～のように見える, ～に似ている **look to** ～しようとする **look up** 見上げる, 調べる

□ **loop** 名 ループ, 輪, 輪状のもの

□ **loose** 形 自由な, ゆるんだ, あいまいな 副 ゆるく

□ **lot of** 熟 《a –》たくさんの～

□ **loving** 形 愛する, 愛情のこもった

□ **lower** 形 もっと低い

□ **lurch** 名 (車などの) がくんとした揺れ, よろめき

□ **lying** 動 lie (横たわる) の現在分詞 形 横になっている

M

□ **mad** 形 ①気の狂った ②逆上した, 理性をなくした

□ **make ～ into** ～を…に仕立てる

□ **make ～ out of …** ～を…から作る

□ **make fun of** ～を物笑いの種にする, からかう

□ **make someone leave** 退職させる

□ **make sure** 確かめる, 確認する

□ **Mako shark** アオザメ

□ **male** 形 男の, 雄の

□ **man-of-war** 名 軍艦, 戦艦

□ **man-of-war bird** グンカンドリ

□ **Manolin** 名 マノーリン《少年の名》

□ **marlin** 名 マカジキ《魚》

□ **mast** 名 マスト, 帆柱

□ **mate** 動 ①交尾する [させる] ②仲間になる, 結婚する

□ **matter** 熟 **not matter** 問題にならない

□ **May I ～?** ～してもよいですか。

□ **meantime** 名 合間, その間 **in**

the meantime それまでは, 当分は

□ **measure** 動 測る

□ **midnight** 名 夜の12時, 真夜中

□ **might** 助《mayの過去》①~かもしれない ②~してもよい, ~できる

□ **mile** 名 マイル《長さの単位。1,609m》

□ **mind** 名 心, 精神, 考え

□ **moment** 名 ①瞬間, ちょっとの間 ②(特定の)時, 時期 **for a moment** 少しの間

□ **more** 熟 **more of** ~よりもっと と **more than** ~以上 **not ~ any more** もう[これ以上]~ない **once more** もう一度

□ **mosquito** 名 カ (蚊)

□ **motionless** 形 動きのない, 静止の

□ **move away** 立ち去る

□ **move off** 立ち去る

□ **movement** 名 動き, 運動

□ **much** 熟 **as much as** ~と同じだけ **too much** 過度の

□ **muscle** 名 筋肉

□ **mutilate** 動 (~を)損傷により損なう, (手足を)切断する

□ **my boy** 息子

N

□ **nearly** 副 ①近くに, 親しく ②ほとんど, あやうく

□ **necessarily** 副 ①必ず, 必然的に, やむを得ず ②《not –》必ずしも~でない

□ **necessary** 形 必要な, 必然の

□ **neither** 形 どちらの~も…でない 代 (2者のうち)どちらも~でない **neither ~ nor …** ~も…もない

□ **news** 名 ニュース, 便り, 知らせ

□ **newspaper** 名 新聞(紙)

□ **next to** ~のとなりに, ~の次に

□ **no** 熟 **do ~ no good** ~に効き目がない **no one** 誰も[一人も]~ない **there is no way** ~する見込みはない

□ **noise** 名 騒音, 騒ぎ, 物音

□ **none** 代 (~の)何も[誰も・少しも]…ない

□ **nonsense** 名 ばかげたこと, ナンセンス

□ **noose** 名 輪なわ

□ **nor** 接 ~もまたない **neither ~ nor …** ~も…もない

□ **normal** 形 普通の, 平均の, 標準的な

□ **northwest** 名 北西(部)

□ **not** 熟 **be not good for** ~に良くない **not matter** 問題にならない **not only ~ but …** ~だけでなく…もまた **not ~ any more** もう[これ以上]~ない **not ~ at all** 少しも[全然]~ない **not ~ but …** ~ではなくて…

□ **note** 動 注意[注目]する

□ **nothing** 熟 **can do nothing** どうしようもない **for nothing** ただで, 無料で, むだに **nothing but** ただ~だけ, ~にすぎない, ~のほかは何も…ない

□ **notice** 動 気づく, 認める

□ **nourish** 動 栄養を与える, 養う

□ **nourishment** 名 滋養, 栄養物, 食物

□ **now** 熟 **now that** 今や~だから, ~からには **right now** 今すぐに, たった今

O

□ **oar** 名 オール, 櫂 (かい)

□ **of course** もちろん, 当然

□ **off** 熟 **move off** 立ち去る **take off**

83

～を取り去る，～を取り除く **tear off**
引きはがす **walk off** 立ち去る

- [ ] **offer** 動 申し出る，提供する
- [ ] **on the surface** 表面で
- [ ] **once more** もう一度
- [ ] **one** 熟 **at one time** ある時には，かつては **each one** 各自 **no one** 誰も［一人も］～ない **one another** お互い **one of** ～の1つ［人］
- [ ] **only** 熟 **not only ～ but …** ～だけでなく…もまた
- [ ] **opening** 動 open（開く）の現在分詞 名 開いた所，穴
- [ ] **ordinary** 形 ①普通の，通常の ②並の，平凡な
- [ ] **original** 形 始めの，元の，本来の
- [ ] **out** 熟 **burn out** 焼き切る **come out** 出てくる，姿を現す **come out of** ～から出てくる **far out** はるか向こうに［で］ **go out** 外出する，外へ出る・出ていく **jump out of** ～から飛び出す **make ～ out of …** ～を…から作る **out of** ①～から外へ，～から抜け出して ②～の範囲外に，～から離れて **out of sight** 見えないところに **spread out** 広げる，展開する **swim out** 泳ぎ出る **take out** 取り出す，取り外す，連れ出す **turn out** ①～と判断する，（結局～に）なる ②（照明などを）消す ③養成する ④出かける，集まる ⑤外側に向く，ひっくり返す
- [ ] **over** 熟 **all over** ～中で，全体に亘って，～の至る所で **be over** 終わる **come over** やって来る **over all** 全体にわたって
- [ ] **overboard** 副 船外へ

P

- [ ] **pack** 名 群れ，一組
- [ ] **paid** 動 pay（払う）の過去，過去分詞

- [ ] **pale** 形 （色が）薄い
- [ ] **palm** 名 手のひら（状のもの）
- [ ] **papa** 名 パパ，お父さん
- [ ] **parent** 名 《-s》両親
- [ ] **pass through** ～を通る，通り抜ける
- [ ] **patch** 名 まだら，斑点
- [ ] **pattern** 名 〔思考や行動などの〕パターン
- [ ] **pay** 動 ①支払う，払う，報いる，償う ②割に合う，ペイする **pay attention to** ～に注意を払う **pay for** ～の対価を払う
- [ ] **pee** 動 おしっこをする
- [ ] **perhaps** 副 たぶん，ことによると
- [ ] **photo** 名 写真
- [ ] **pick up** 拾い上げる
- [ ] **pillow** 名 まくら
- [ ] **pinch** 動 つまむ，はさむ
- [ ] **planking** 名 板張り
- [ ] **pleasant** 形 ①（物事が）楽しい，心地よい ②快活な，愛想のよい
- [ ] **porpoise** 名 ネズミイルカ
- [ ] **pound** 名 ポンド《重量の単位。453.6g》 動 どんどんたたく，打ち砕く
- [ ] **pour** 動 注ぐ
- [ ] **prayer** 名 祈り，祈願（文）
- [ ] **press** 動 圧する，押す，プレスする
- [ ] **pressure** 名 プレッシャー，圧力，圧縮
- [ ] **price** 名 値段
- [ ] **pride** 名 誇り，自慢，自尊心
- [ ] **probably** 副 たぶん，あるいは
- [ ] **project** 動 突き出る
- [ ] **proprietor** 名 持ち主，所有者
- [ ] **pull in** 引っ込める，（網，釣り糸を）引く
- [ ] **pull on** ～を引っ張る，こぎ続ける

□ **pull up** 引っ張り上げる

□ **punch** 動 げんこつでなぐる

□ **punishment** 名 ①罰, 処罰 ②罰を受けること

□ **purple** 形 紫色の 名 紫色

□ **push against** ～で…を押す

□ **push back** 押し返す, 押しのける

□ **put ～ into ...** ～を…の状態にする, ～を…に突っ込む

□ **put down** 下に置く, 下ろす

□ **put in** ～の中に入れる

□ **put on** ①～を身につける, 着る ②～を…の上に置く

□ **pyramid-shaped** 形 ピラミッド型をした

Q

□ **quality** 名 ①質, 性質, 品質 ②特性 ③良質

□ **quarter** 名 4分の1

□ **quickly** 副 敏速に, 急いで

□ **quietly** 副 ①静かに ②平穏に, 控えめに

R

□ **radio** 名 ラジオ

□ **raise** 動 ①(持ち)上げる ②立たせる, 起こす

□ **rather** 副 ①むしろ, かえって ②かなり, いくぶん, やや ③それどころか逆に **would rather** ～する方がよい

□ **raw** 形 生の, 未加工の

□ **razor-sharp** 形 かみそりのように鋭い

□ **reach for** ～に手を伸ばす, ～を取ろうとする

□ **realize** 動 理解する, 実現する

□ **recognize** 動 認める, 認識[承認]する

□ **reflected** 形 映し出された

□ **reflection** 名 反射, (鏡・水などに)映った姿, 映像

□ **relax** 動 ①くつろがせる ②ゆるめる, 緩和する

□ **release** 動 解き放す

□ **religious** 形 信心深い

□ **resolution** 名 ①決定, 決議 ②決心, 決断

□ **respect** 動 尊敬[尊重]する

□ **reverse** 動 逆にする, 覆す

□ **right now** 今すぐに, たった今

□ **rip** 動 引き裂く, 切り裂く, 破る

□ **rise to one's feet** 立ち上がる

□ **risen** 動 rise (昇る) の過去分詞

□ **rode** 動 ride (乗る) の過去

□ **Rogelio** 名 ロヘリオ《人名》

□ **roll** 動 (～を) 巻く **roll up** 巻き上げる

□ **rounded** 形 曲線的な, 丸みを帯びた

□ **row** 名 (横に並んだ) 列 **a row of** 1列の～ 動 (舟を) こぐ

□ **rub** 動 こする

□ **rudder** 名 舵 (かじ)

□ **ruin** 動 破滅させる

□ **run down** (液体が) 流れ落ちる, 駆け下りる

□ **run through** 走り抜ける

□ **rush** 動 突進する, せき立てる **rush out** どっと出てくる, 性急に出ていく 名 突進, 突撃, 殺到 **in a rush** 大急ぎで

S

□ **sack** 名 〔粗い布製の〕ずだ袋《ジャガイモ, 石炭, コーヒーなどを運ぶも

85

- [ ] **sail** 名①帆, 帆船 ②帆走, 航海 **set sail** 出帆［出航］する 動帆走する, 航海する, 出航する
- [ ] **same ~ as ...**《the－》…と同じ（ような）~
- [ ] **sand flea** スナノミ
- [ ] **sank** 動sink (沈む) の過去
- [ ] **Santiago** 名サンチャゴ《老漁師の名》
- [ ] **sardine** 名イワシ (鰯)《魚》
- [ ] **say to oneself** ひとり言を言う, 心に思う
- [ ] **scar** 名傷跡
- [ ] **scavenger** 名①ごみをあさる人 ②腐肉を食べる動物
- [ ] **scent** 名①(快い) におい, 香り ②手がかり
- [ ] **scoop** 動すくい上げる, かき集める
- [ ] **search** 動捜し求める
- [ ] **seawater** 名海水
- [ ] **seaweed** 名海藻, 海草
- [ ] **see ~ as ...** ~を…と考える
- [ ] **see if** ~かどうかを確かめる
- [ ] **seem** 動(~に) 見える, (~のように) 思われる
- [ ] **serve** 動食事［飲み物］を出す
- [ ] **set sail** 出帆［出航］する
- [ ] **set to** ~へ向かう, ~に着手する, けんかを始める, 食べ始める, 本気で始める
- [ ] **setting** 名〔月や太陽が〕沈むこと
- [ ] **settle** 動安定する［させる］, 落ち着く, 落ち着かせる
- [ ] **shack** 名掘っ立て小屋
- [ ] **shadow** 名影
- [ ] **shaft** 名柄
- [ ] **shake** 動振る, 揺れる, 揺さぶる, 震える

- [ ] **shaking** 名振動
- [ ] **shaped** 形~の形をした
- [ ] **shark** 名サメ (鮫)
- [ ] **sharp** 形鋭い, とがった
- [ ] **sharpen** 動鋭くする, 鋭くなる, とぐ
- [ ] **sharply** 副鋭く, 激しく, はっきりと
- [ ] **sheet** 名(紙などの) 1枚
- [ ] **shell** 名〔カニ・エビ・昆虫などの〕殻, 甲羅
- [ ] **shift** 動移す, 変える, 転嫁する
- [ ] **shining** 形光る, 輝く, きらめく
- [ ] **shiver** 動(寒さなどで) 身震いする, 震える
- [ ] **shone** 動shine (光る) の過去, 過去分詞
- [ ] **shook** 動shake (振る) の過去
- [ ] **shore** 名岸, 海岸, 陸
- [ ] **shorten** 動短くする, 縮める
- [ ] **should have done** ~すべきだった (のにしなかった)《仮定法》
- [ ] **shoulder** 名肩
- [ ] **shovel-nose** 名シャベルのような鼻
- [ ] **shovel-nosed shark** シャベルのような鼻をしたサメ《ここではメジロザメ科のニシレモンザメ (lemon shark) のこと》
- [ ] **shovel-pointed** 形シャベルの先のような
- [ ] **shrimp** 名小エビ, シュリンプ
- [ ] **shrug** 動(肩を) すくめる
- [ ] **shut** ①閉まる, 閉める, 閉じる ②たたむ ③閉じ込める ④shutの過去, 過去分詞
- [ ] **sick** 熟feel sick 気分が悪い
- [ ] **sickness** 名病気
- [ ] **side** 名側, 横, そば, 斜面 **side by side** 並んで
- [ ] **sideways** 副横(向き) に, 斜めに

□ **sight** 熟 out of sight 見えないところに

□ **silly** 形 おろかな, 思慮のない

□ **silver** 形 銀色をした

□ **silvery** 形 銀のような

□ **simply** 副 ①簡単に ②単に, ただ

□ **sin** 名 (道徳・宗教上の)罪

□ **single** 形 単独の

□ **sink** 動 沈む

□ **sit up** 起き上がる, 上半身を起こす

□ **skeleton** 名 骨格, がい骨, 骨組み

□ **slam** 動 激しく打つ, たたきつける

□ **slant** 動 傾く, 傾ける, 傾斜する

□ **slap** 動 (平手, 平たいもので)ぴしゃりと打つ

□ **slave** 名 奴隷 slave work 奴隷のような労働[仕事]

□ **slice** 名 薄切りの1枚, 部分

□ **slid** 動 slide (滑る)の過去, 過去分詞

□ **slide** 動 滑る, 滑らせる, 滑って行く

□ **slip** 動 滑る, 滑らせる, 滑って転ぶ slip away すり抜ける, こっそり去る, 静かに立ち去る

□ **slit** 動 細長く切る

□ **slitted** 形 切れ長の, 長く裂けた

□ **slowly** 副 遅く, ゆっくり

□ **smooth** 形 滑らかな, すべすべした

□ **snap** 動 ①ぽきっと折る, ぶつんと切る ②ぱたんと閉じる[閉まる]

□ **so** 熟 and so そこで, それだから, それで so far 今までのところ, これまでは so that ～するために, それで, ～できるように

□ **soak** 動 浸す, 浸る

□ **softly** 副 柔らかに, 優しく, そっと

□ **some** 熟 for some time しばらくの間 in some way 何とかして, 何らかの方法で some time いつか, そのうち

□ **somehow** 副 ①どうにかこうにか, ともかく, 何とかして ②どういうわけか

□ **someone** 代 ある人, 誰か

□ **something** 代 ①ある物, 何か ②いくぶん, 多少

□ **sometimes** 副 時々, 時たま

□ **sore** 形 痛い, 傷のある

□ **sorry** 熟 feel sorry for ～をかわいそうに思う

□ **southwest** 副 南西へ

□ **spat** 動 spit (吐く)の過去, 過去分詞

□ **spear** 名 槍, 銛(ふん)

□ **speed** 名 速力, 速度 動 加速する, 速める speed up 加速する

□ **speedboat** 名 スピードボート

□ **spine** 名 脊柱, 脊椎骨

□ **splash** 名 (泥などの)はね, ざぶんという音

□ **spot** 名 ①地点, 場所, 立場 ②斑点, しみ

□ **spray** 名 スプレー

□ **spread out** 広げる, 展開する

□ **squarely** 副 四角に, 公正に

□ **stab** 動 (突き)刺す

□ **stack** 動 積み重ねる

□ **stand up** 立ち上がる

□ **stay with** ～に付き添う

□ **steal** 動 盗む

□ **steer** 動 舵をとる, 操縦する

□ **stern** 名 船尾

□ **stick** 名 棒, 棒切れ

□ **stiff** 形 堅い, こわばった

□ **stone** 名 砥石

□ **stoop** 動 かがむ

□ **straighten** 動 まっすぐにする[なる] straighten up 体を真っすぐに立てる, 立ち上がる, 体[上体を]起こ

87

す

□ **strangeness** 名不思議

□ **straw** 名麦わら, ストロー

□ **stream** 名流れ

□ **strength** 名力, 体力

□ **stripe** 名筋, 縞, ストライプ

□ **struck** 動 strike (打つ) の過去, 過去分詞

□ **stuff** 名①材料, 原料 ②もの, 持ち物

□ **stupid** 形ばかな, おもしろくない

□ **submerge** 動沈める, 水中に入れる

□ **successful** 形成功した, うまくいった

□ **such a** そのような

□ **such as** たとえば~, ~のような

□ **sucking fish** コバンザメ《魚》

□ **sudden** 形突然の, 急な

□ **suffer** 動①(苦痛・損害などを) 受ける, こうむる ②(病気に) なる, 苦しむ, 悩む

□ **sunrise** 名日の出

□ **sunset** 名日没, 夕焼け

□ **suppose** 動①仮定する, 推測する ②《be -d to ~》~することになっている, ~するものである

□ **sure** 熟 make sure 確かめる, 確認する

□ **surface** 名①表面, 水面 ②うわべ, 外見 on the surface 表面で

□ **swallow** 動①飲み込む ②うのみにする

□ **swam** 動 swim (泳ぐ) の過去

□ **sweat** 名汗 動汗をかく

□ **sweeping** 弧 [カーブ] を描く

□ **swim out** 泳ぎ出る

□ **sword** 名剣, 刀

□ **swordfish** 名メカジキ《名》

□ **swung** 動 swing (回転する) の過去,

過去分詞

T

□ **tail** 名尾, しっぽ

□ **take** 熟 take down 下げる, 降ろす take hold of ~をつかむ, 捕らえる, 制する take off ~を取り去る, ~を取り除く take out 取り出す, 取り外す, 連れ出す take someone home ~を家へ持って帰る take someone in ~を迎え入れる take up 取り上げる, 拾い上げる take ~ to … ~を…に連れて行く

□ **taste** 名味, 風味 動味がする, 味わう

□ **tear off** 引きはがす

□ **tender** 形柔らかい

□ **tension** 名緊張(関係), ぴんと張ること

□ **terrace** 名テラス

□ **than** 熟 more than ~以上

□ **that** 熟 after that その後 now that 今や~だから, ~からには so that ~するために, それで, ~できるように

□ **then** 熟 just then そのとたんに

□ **there is no way** ~する見込みはない

□ **these days** このごろ

□ **thigh** 名太もも, 大腿部

□ **thin** 形薄い, 細い, やせた

□ **think of** ~のことを考える, ~を思いつく, 考え出す

□ **this** 熟 at this これを見て, そこで (すぐに) like this このような, こんなふうに

□ **though** 接①~にもかかわらず, ~だが ②たとえ~でも as though あたかも~のように, まるで~みたいに even though ~であるけれども, ~にもかかわらず 副しかし

- **Three-quarters** 名 4分の3
- **through** 熟 pass through ～を通る, 通り抜ける run through 走り抜ける
- **thumb** 名 親指
- **tiburon** 名 ティブロン；サメ《スペイン語》
- **tide** 名 潮, 潮流
- **tight** 形 堅い, きつい, ぴんと張った 副 堅く, しっかりと
- **tighten** 動 ぴんと張る, 堅く締める
- **tiller** 名 舵の柄
- **time** 熟 all the time ずっと, いつも, その間ずっと at one time ある時には, かつては each time ～するたびに for some time しばらくの間 some time いつか, そのうち
- **tiny** 形 ちっぽけな, とても小さい
- **tired** 形 ①疲れた, くたびれた ②あきた, うんざりした
- **together** 熟 be held together with ～でとめられている [結び付けられている]
- **too ～ to ...** …するには～すぎる
- **too good to last** 良いことは長く続かない
- **too much** 過度の
- **tore** 動 tear (裂く) の過去
- **toss** 動 投げる, 放り上げる
- **tourist** 名 旅行者, 観光客
- **tow** 動 (車・船などをロープで) 引く, 曳航する
- **trace** 名 ①跡 ②(事件などの) こん跡
- **triangular** 形 三角 (形) の
- **trick** 名 策略
- **truly** 副 ①全く, 本当に, 真に ②心から, 誠実に
- **tuna** 名 マグロ (鮪)
- **turn around** 振り向く, 向きを変える, 方向転換する

- **turn on** ①～の方を向く ②(スイッチなどを) ひねってつける, 出す
- **turn out** ①～と判明する, (結局～に) なる ②(照明などを) 消す ③養成する ④出かける, 集まる ⑤外側に向く, ひっくり返す
- **turtle** 名 ウミガメ (海亀)
- **twist** 動 ①ねじる, よれる ②身をよじる

U

- **unarmed** 形 武器を用いない
- **unavoidable** 形 避けられない
- **unclear** 形 明確でない, はっきりしない
- **undefeated** 形 不屈の
- **understanding** 形 理解のある, 思いやりのある
- **unless** 接 もし～でなければ, ～しなければ
- **untie** 動 ほどく, 解放する
- **up and down** 上がったり下がったり, 行ったり来たり, あちこちと
- **up to** ～まで, ～に至るまで, ～に匹敵して
- **us** 熟 let us どうか私たちに～させてください
- **used** 動 ①use (使う) の過去, 過去分詞 ②《 – to》よく～したものだ, 以前は～であった 形 ①慣れている, 《get [become] – to》～に慣れてくる ②使われた, 中古の
- **useless** 形 役に立たない, 無益な
- **usual** 形 通常の, いつもの, 平常の, 普通の

V

- **very well** 結構, よろしい
- **violet** 形 スミレ色の

□ **visible** 形目に見える, 明らかな

W

□ **wait for** ～を待つ

□ **waiter** 名ウェイター, 給仕

□ **wake up** 起きる, 目を覚ます

□ **walk off** 立ち去る

□ **walk up** 歩み寄る, 歩いて上る

□ **wall** 熟 **against the wall** 壁を背にして

□ **wave** 名波

□ **way** 熟 **all the way** ずっと, はるばる, いろいろと **in some way** 何とかして, 何らかの方法で **one's way (to ～)** (～への) 途中で **there is no way to ～** ～する見込みはない **way to ～** する方法

□ **weapon** 名武器

□ **weave** 動織る, 編む

□ **weight** 名重さ, 重力, 体重

□ **well** 熟 **as well** なお, その上, 同様に **as well as** ～と同様に **get well** (病気が) よくなる **very well** 結構, よろしい

□ **wet** 形ぬれた, 湿った 動ぬらす, ぬれる

□ **what ～ for** どんな目的で

□ **while** 熟 **after a while** しばらくして

□ **white-tipped** 形先端が白い

□ **Who knows?** 誰にわかるだろうか。誰にもわからない。

□ **whole** 形全体の, すべての, 完全な, 満～, 丸～

□ **Why not?** どうしてだめなのですか。いいですとも。ぜひそうしよう！

□ **wide** 形幅の広い, 広範囲の, 幅が～ある 副広く, 大きく開いて

□ **widen** 動広くなる [する], 大きく開く

□ **width** 名幅, 広さ

□ **will have done** ～してしまっているだろう《未来完了形》

□ **wind up** (ネジ・ぜんまいなどを) 巻き上げる

□ **wing** 名翼, 羽

□ **wipe** 動～をふく, ぬぐう, ふきとる

□ **wish** 熟 **I wish ～ were** … 私が～なら …なのに。《仮定法過去》

□ **withdrew** 動 withdraw (引っ込める) の過去

□ **without** 熟 **go without** ～なしですませる

□ **woke** 動 wake (目が覚める) の過去

□ **wonder** 動 ①不思議に思う, (～に) 驚く ②(～かしらと) 思う

□ **wooden** 形木製の, 木でできた

□ **work on** ～で働く, ～に取り組む

□ **worried** 動 worry (悩む) の過去, 過去分詞 形心配そうな, 不安げな

□ **worthless** 形価値のない, 役立たずの

□ **worthy** 形価値のある, 立派な

□ **would have … if ～** もし～だったとしたら…しただろう

□ **would like to** ～したいと思う

□ **would rather** ～する方がよい

□ **wound** 名傷

□ **wrinkle** 名しわ

Y

□ **year** 熟 **for years** 何年も

English Conversational Ability Test
国際英語会話能力検定

● E-CATとは…
英語が話せるようになるための
テストです。インターネット
ベースで、30分であなたの発
話力をチェックします。

www.ecatexam.com

● iTEP®とは…
世界各国の企業、政府機関、アメリカの大学
300校以上が、英語能力判定テストとして採用。
オンラインによる90分のテストで文法、リー
ディング、リスニング、ライティング、スピー
キングの5技能をスコア化。iTEP®は、留学、就
職、海外赴任などに必要な、世界に通用する英
語力を総合的に評価する画期的なテストです。

www.itepexamjapan.com

ラダーシリーズ

The Old Man and the Sea 老人と海

2022年1月8日　第1刷発行
2022年5月27日　第2刷発行

原著者　アーネスト・ヘミングウェイ

発行者　浦　晋亮

発行所　**IBCパブリッシング株式会社**
　　　　〒162-0804 東京都新宿区中里町29番3号
　　　　菱秀神楽坂ビル
　　　　Tel. 03-3513-4511　Fax. 03-3513-4512
　　　　www.ibcpub.co.jp

印　刷　株式会社シナノパブリッシングプレス
装　丁　伊藤　理恵
イラスト　ミヤザーナツ

Printed in Japan
ISBN978-4-7946-0690-7